if ONly You KNEW HoW MUCH You Are WORTH

LEA EALUM

ILLUSTRATED BY DEBBIE NEAU

iUniverse books may be ordered through booksellers or by contacting:

iUniverse
1663 Liberty Drive
Bloomington, IN 47403
www.iuniverse.com
1-800-Authors (1-800-288-4677)

Because of the dynamic nature of the Internet, any web addresses or links contained in this book may have changed since publication and may no longer be valid. The views expressed in this work are solely those of the author and do not necessarily reflect the views of the publisher, and the publisher hereby disclaims any responsibility for them.

Any people depicted in stock imagery provided by Getty Images are models,
and such images are being used for illustrative purposes only.
Certain stock imagery © Getty Images.

ISBN: 978-1-5320-7299-4 (sc)
ISBN: 978-1-5320-7301-4 (hc)
ISBN: 978-1-5320-7300-7 (e)

Library of Congress Control Number: 2019904124

Print information available on the last page.

iUniverse rev. date: 05/03/2019

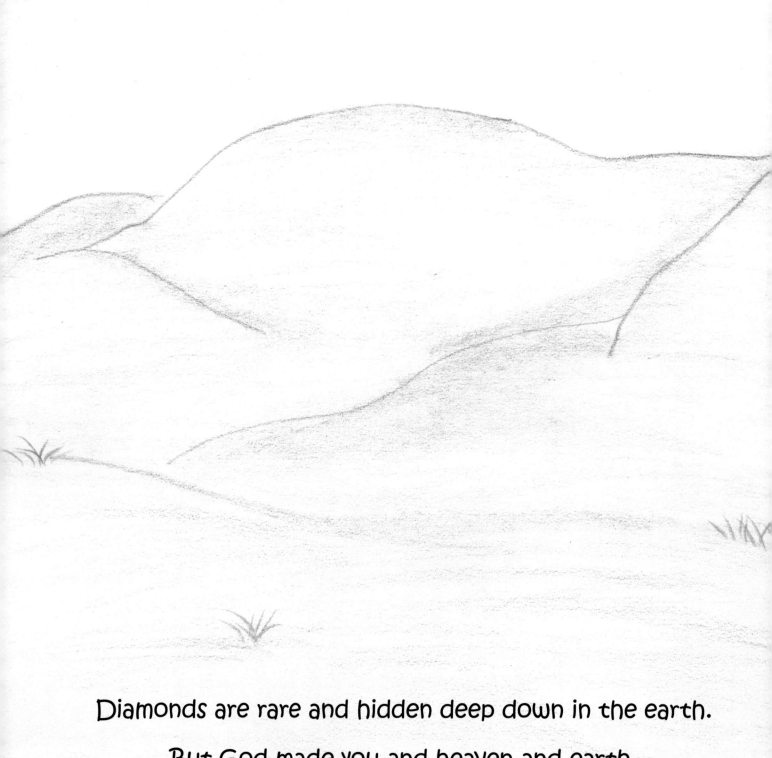

Diamonds are rare and hidden deep down in the earth.

But God made you and heaven and earth.

If only you knew how much you are worth.

Gold shines bright and fetches a high price.

But God made you to shine like a light.

If only you knew how much you are worth.

Matthew 5:16

Pearls are harvested from the depths of the sea.

We string them together to make pretty things.

But you are worth more than all the pearls in the sea.

Yes, you are worth more than anything.

Matthew 13:45-46

You are remarkably and wonderfully made.

You were made by the hands of the King.

He only chose the finest of things.

Psalms 139:14

Your skin color was chosen just for you.

Your eyes, your nose, and your ears too.

Psalms 139:15

Your hairs were all counted and arranged just right.

There is not another one like you in sight.

Luke 12:7

The mighty King that made everything,

made you like him in so many ways.

But you were given freewill and began to stray,

And just like that you went your own way.

The King didn't need you but loved
you and wanted you home.

So, he sent his son, Jesus, who left his throne.

Matthew 1:21

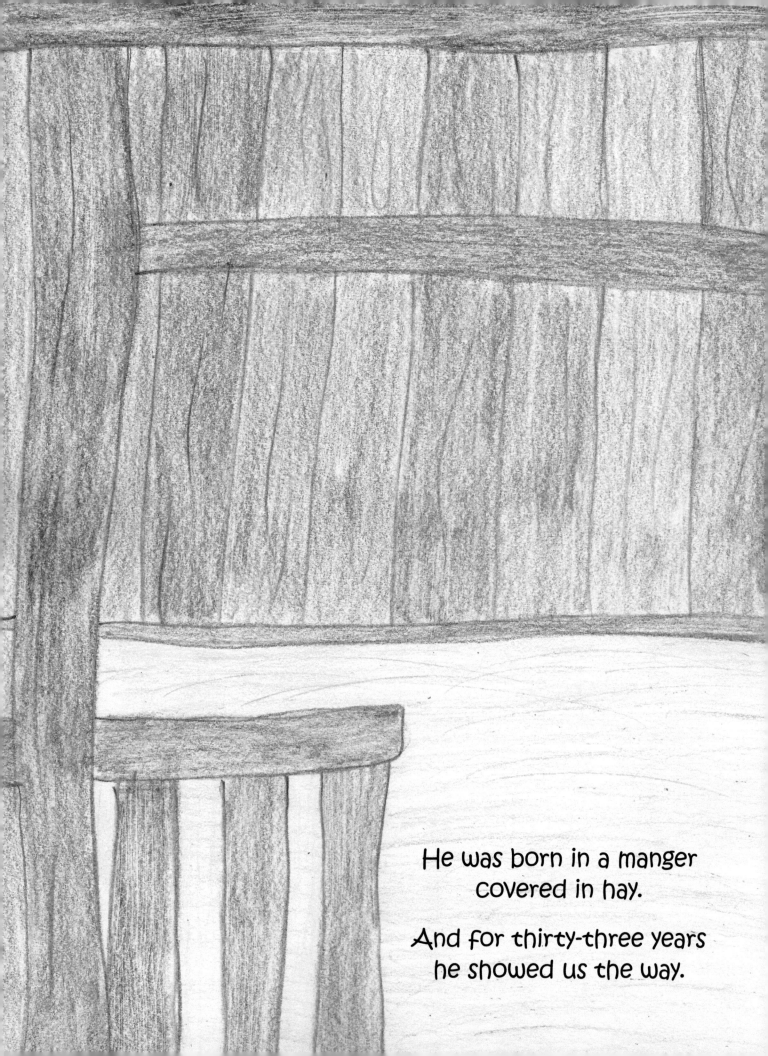

He was born in a manger
covered in hay.

And for thirty-three years
he showed us the way.

Matthew 22: 37-39

Jesus paid for our sins so we would not be lost.

He was mocked, beaten, and died on a cross.

Yes, this was great,

and a price that was tall.

But when King Jesus rose, he saved us all.

Romans 10:9

So in all you do and wherever you go, the King is with you, this you must know.

You are loved, wanted, and bought with a price.

And paid for by the blood of Christ.

Acts 2:38

So sons and daughters of the mighty King,

remember you are worth more than anything.

John 3:16

Zephaniah 3:17

Jeremiah 29:11-12

Printed in the United States
By Bookmasters